Bond

Verbal Reasoning

Assessment Papers

8–9 years

J M Bond
Frances Down

OXFORD
UNIVERSITY PRESS

UNIVERSITY PRESS

Great Clarendon Street, Oxford, OX2 6DP, United Kingdom

Oxford University Press is a department of the University of Oxford. It furthers the University's objective of excellence in research, scholarship, and education by publishing worldwide. Oxford is a registered trade mark of Oxford University Press in the UK and in certain other countries

First published in 2002 by Nelson Thornes Ltd
This edition published in 2014

British Library Cataloguing in Publication Data
Data available

978-1-4085-2516-6

10 9 8 7 6 5 4 3 2

Printed in Great Britain by Ashford Colour Press Ltd

Page make-up by OKS Prepress, India

Before you get started

What is Bond?

This book is part of the Bond Assessment Papers series for verbal reasoning, which provides a **thorough and continuous course in verbal reasoning** from ages six to twelve. It builds up verbal reasoning skills from book to book over the course of the series.

What does this book cover?

Verbal reasoning questions can be grouped into four distinct groups: sorting words, selecting words, anagrams, coded sequences and logic. This book practises a wide range of questions appropriate to the age group drawn from all these categories. One of the key features of Bond Assessment Papers is that each one practises **a very wide variety of skills and question types** so that children are always challenged to think – and don't get bored repeating the same question type again and again. We believe that variety is the key to effective learning. It helps children 'think on their feet' and cope with the unexpected.

The age given on the cover is for guidance only. As the papers are designed to be reasonably challenging for the age group, any one child may naturally find him or herself working above or below the stated age. The important thing is that children are always encouraged by their performance. Working at the right level is the key to this.

What does the book contain?

- **20 papers** – each one contains 45 questions.
- **Scoring devices** – there are score boxes next to the questions and a Progress Chart at the back. The chart is a visual and motivating way for children to see how they are doing. Encouraging them to colour in the chart as they go along and to try to beat their last score can be highly effective!
- **Next Steps Planner** – advice on what to do after finishing the papers can be found on the inside back cover.
- **Answers** – located in an easily-removed central pull-out section.

How can you use this book?

One of the great strengths of Bond Assessment Papers is their flexibility. They can be used at home, school and by tutors to:

- provide regular verbal reasoning practice in **bite-sized chunks**
- **highlight strengths and weaknesses** in the core skills
- identify **individual needs**
- set **homework**
- set **timed formal practice tests** – allow about 30 minutes.

It is best to start at the beginning and work through the papers in order.

What does a score mean and how can it be improved?

If children colour in the Progress Chart at the back, this will give an idea of how they are doing. The Next Steps Planner inside the back cover will help you to decide what to do next to help a child progress. We suggest that it is always valuable to go over any wrong answers with children.

Don't forget the website…!

Visit www.assessmentpapers.co.uk for lots of advice, information and suggestions on everything to do with Bond, helping children to do their best, and exams.

Paper 1

Underline the pair of words most similar in meaning.

Example come, go   <u>roam, wander</u>   fear, fare

1 <u>alley, lane</u>   real, false   back, forward

2 good, bad   bake, oven   <u>heavy, weighty</u>

3 beat, lose   <u>bite, nip</u>   bath, room

4 nose, face   shallow, river   <u>correct, right</u>

5 come, go   sorry, glad   <u>closed, shut</u>

5

Find the three-letter word which can be added to the letters in capitals to make a new word. The new word will complete the sentence sensibly.

Example The cat sprang onto the MO.   <u>USE</u>

6 SN days make a week.   *eve*

7 We put SS on our feet.   *hoe*

8 He FED his cup to the brim.   *ill*

9 They SED me the way to the town.   *how*

10 I would like to hear a story BEE I go to sleep.   *for*

5

Underline two words, one from each group, that go together to form a new word. The word in the first group always comes first.

Example (hand, <u>green</u>, for)   (light, <u>house</u>, sure)

11 (is, <u>be</u>, it)   (bed, <u>low</u>, high)

12 (shut, open, <u>in</u>)   (<u>side</u>, back, air)

13 (<u>for</u>, form, fear)   (car, <u>got</u>, back)

14 (toe, <u>finger</u>, hand)   (rip, <u>tip</u>, side)

15 (face, hair, <u>hand</u>)   (shave, <u>some</u>, were)

5

(1)

Change the first word of the third pair in the same way as the other pairs to give a new word.

Example bind, hind   bare, hare   but, <u>hut</u>

16 art, part   ale, pale   ant, _part_
17 ill, till   all, tall   ear, _tear_
18 pick, prick   feed, freed   tied, _tried_
19 ran, rain   man, main   pan _pain_
20 top, stop   tar, star   tab, _stab_

5

Fill in the missing letters. The alphabet has been written out to help you.

A B C D E F G H I J K L M N O P Q R S T U V W X Y Z

Example   AB is to CD as PQ is to <u>RS</u>.

21 A is to D as G is to _J_.
22 3B is to 4D as 5F is to _6H_.
23 ABD is to BCE as CDF is to _DEG_.
24 MAB is to NBC as OCD is to _PDE_.
25 9AB is to 8CD as 7EF is to _6GH_

5

Fill in the crosswords so that all the given words are included. You have been given one letter as a clue in each crossword.

26

h	o	m	e
i	■	■	d
n	■	■	i
t	e	n	t

edit, hint, home, tent

27

t	e	r	m
i	■	■	o
M	■	■	s
e	n	d	s

ends, moss, term, time

28

w	i	s	h
a	■	■	e
g	■	■	a
S	H	i	p

heap, ship, wags, wish

3

Fill in the missing number in each sequence.

Example   2   4   6   8   <u>10</u>

29 12   15   _____   21   24

30 1996   1998   _____   2002   2004

31 20   17   14   11   _____

32 4.5   5.0   5.5   6.0   _____

33 19   _____   22   25   29

34 20   18   15   11   _____

( ) 6

If the code for PEARS is 13579, what are the codes for the following words?

35 ARE _____   **36** RAP _____

37 SPA _____   **38** SEE _____

39 PEA _____

What do these codes stand for?

40 91357 _____   **41** 511357 _____

( ) 7

Here are some TV programmes.

> 14:00 Play School
>
> 14:15 Cartoons
>
> 15:30 Think Twice
>
> 16:00 The School on the Hill
>
> 16:30 News

How many minutes do these programmes last?

42 Play School __ minutes **43** Cartoons __ minutes

44 Think Twice __ minutes **45** The School on the Hill __ minutes

( ) 4

Paper 2

Underline the word in brackets closest in meaning to the word in capitals.

1 CLEVER   (school   bright   pupil   stupid   trick)   ✓

2 QUICK   (slow   fast   speed   walk   step)   ✓

3 LAUGH   (cry   taught   funny   chuckle   humour)   ✓

4 MODERN   (easy   today   young   new   trend)   ✓

5 SIMPLE   (crazy   silly   hard   easy   straight)   ✓   5 5

Find the missing number by using the two numbers outside the brackets in the same way as the other sets of numbers.

Example   2 [8] 4   3 [18] 6   5 [25] 5

6   3 [9] 6   4 [6] 2   1 [6] 6   ✗

7   5 [10] 2   4 [12] 3   6 [12] 2   ✓

8   2 [5] 3   7 [8] 1   2 [16] 8   ✗

9   7 [6] 1   5 [3] 2   8 [32] 4   ✗

10 15 [5] 3   21 [3] 7   16 [4] 4   ✗   1 5

Find the letter which will end the first word and start the second word.

Example   peac (h) ome

11 han (d) oor   ✓

12 mat (t) ver   ✓

13 sal (t) ill   ✓

14 duc (k) ite   ✓

15 mas (t) est   ✓   5 5

Fill in the crosswords so that all the given words are included. You have been given one letter as a clue in each crossword.

16

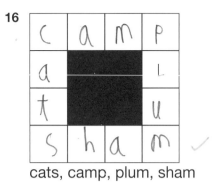

C	a	m	P
a	■	■	L
t	■	■	u
S	h	a	m

cats, camp, plum, sham

17

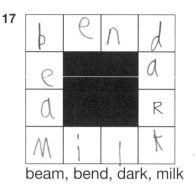

b	e	n	d
e	■	■	a
a	■	■	R
M	i	l	k

beam, bend, dark, milk

18

b	a	n	k
e	■	■	i
A	■	■	n
r	i	n	g

bank, bear, king, ring

Underline two words, one from each group, that go together to form a new word. The word in the first group always comes first.

Example (hand, <u>green</u>, for) (light, <u>house</u>, sure)

19 (bed, for, right) (tub, cot, side)

20 (near, after, under) (some, ground, set)

21 (in, an, it) (left, form, just)

22 (far, near, out) (law, police, here)

23 (far, for, ran) (take, give, us)

Change the first word into the last word by changing one letter at a time and making a new word in the middle.

Example CASE _CASH_ LASH

24 PANE _Pine_ PINK

25 COMB _Come_ HOME

5

26 HOPE   *Cope*   COPY ✓

27 HATE   *Mate*   MITE ✓

28 COLD   *Gold*   GILD ✓

If the code for POSTER is 235689, what are the codes for the following words?

29 STOP _5632_ ✓   30 SET _586_ ✓

What do these codes stand for?

31 632   *TOP* ✓   32 6355   *TOSS* ✓

33 899   *ERR* ✓

Choose the word or phrase that makes each sentence true.

Example   A LIBRARY always has (posters, a carpet, <u>books</u>, DVDs, stairs).

34 A HOUSE always has (a garage, curtains, (walls) a doorbell, a fence). ✓

35 A LAKE always has (ducks, boats, fish, swans, (water)) ✓

36 A CITY always has (farms, (buildings) an airport, an underground, a river). ✓

37 A KITCHEN always has (a table, chairs, (a stove) plants, a radio). ✓

38 A SCHOOL always has (a cafeteria, a nurse, (students) a swimming pool, a bus). ✓

Underline the two words which are made from the same letters.

Example   TAP   PET   <u>TEA</u>   POT   <u>EAT</u>

39 (MEAT)   TIME   TUNE   (TEAM)   MUST ✓

40 NUT   (TEN)   (NET)   TAN   NOT ✓

41 TEST   STAB   (LAST)   LOST   (SALT) ✓

6

Remove one letter from the word in capitals to leave a new word. The meaning of the new word is given in the clue.

Example   AUNT   an insect   <u>ant</u>

42 FARM   not near   _Far_   ✓

43 HARM   a piece of meat   _Ham_   ✓

44 GROUND   shaped like a ball   _Round_   ✓

45 THAN   you get it from sunbathing   _Tan_   ✓   4

Now go to the Progress Chart to record your score!   Total   45

Paper 3

Underline the two words which are the odd ones out in the following groups of words.

Example   black   <u>king</u>   purple   green   <u>house</u>

1 quiet   peaceful   crowd   calm   concert

2 small   short   enlarge   brief   expand

3 sea   harbour   ocean   pier   lake

4 sturdy   weak   strong   healthy   ill

5 walk   swim   stride   dive   march   5

Find the three-letter word which can be added to the letters in capitals to make a new word. The new word will complete the sentence sensibly.

Example   The cat sprang onto the MO.   <u>USE</u>

6 The weather was W and sunny.   _____

7 He SCHED high and low for the remote control.   _____

8 I've got some nice, new PYAS to wear.   _____

9 My favourite fruit is an APRI.   _____

10 The octopus caught him with its TACLES.   _____   5

Which one letter can be added to the front of all of these words to make new words?

Example   care   cat   crate   call

11   __late   __lease   __ony   __each

12   __right   __ig   __all   __ean

13   __how   __et   __poon   __nake

14   __elt   __eal   __at   __oan

15   __hall   __eal   __mall   __nail

⬤ 5

Add one letter to the word in capital letters to make a new word. The meaning of the new word is given in the clue.

Example   PLAN   simple   plain

16   TROT   a fish   _____

17   NOSE   the opposite of silence   _____

18   TICK   the opposite of thin   _____

19   LATE   used to put our food on   _____

20   SORT   different types of games   _____

⬤ 5

Fill in the crosswords so that all the given words are included. You have been given one letter as a clue in each crossword.

21
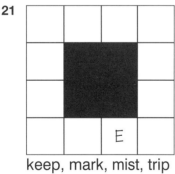
keep, mark, mist, trip

22
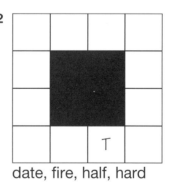
date, fire, half, hard

23
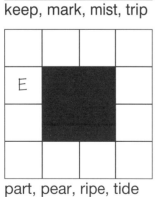
part, pear, ripe, tide

⬤ 3

Fill in the missing number in each sequence.

Example   2   4   6   8   _10_

24   3   6   9   —   15

25   12   10   8   —   4

26   12   24   —   48   60

27   21   32   43   —   65

28   121   232   —   454   565

These words have been written in code, but the codes are not under the right words.

TOO   OUT   TOT   TO   UP

72   722   247   46   727

Write the correct code for each word.

29 TOO   _____   **30** OUT   _____

31 TOT   _____   **32** TO   _____

33 UP   _____

If a = 1, b = 2, c = 3, find the sum of:

34 a + b + c = _____   **35** c + 2b = _____

36 2a + 2b = _____

Underline the one word which **cannot be made** from the letters of the word in capital letters.

Example   STATIONERY   stones   tyres   ration   <u>nation</u>   noisy

37 CONSIDER   cried   nice   dear   rice   coin

38 LOWEST   low   west   flow   sew   owl

39 TEACHER   eaten   chat   ear   are   crate

40 INSIDE   den   snide   end   dine   need

In each line, underline the word that has its letters in alphabetical order.

41 gas   guzzle   grunt   got

42 apple   ant   ask   ale

43 clever   caution   care   cry

44 deal   dint   dream   drink

45 flow   flea   frank   frog   5

Now go to the Progress Chart to record your score!   Total   45

Paper 4

Find and underline the two words which need to change places for each sentence to make sense.

Example She went to <u>letter</u> the <u>write</u>.

1 The tail wagged her dog when she saw the treat.

2 My sister told my mother to finish her homework.

3 I like to read a bed before book.

4 At my birthday cake we ate ice cream and party.

5 My mum takes the office to her bus.   5

Underline two words, one from each group, that go together to form a new word. The word in the first group always comes first.

Example (hand, <u>green</u>, for)   (light, <u>house</u>, sure)

6 (wood, light, sea)   (day, tree, weed)

7 (earth, glass, sand)   (sun, castle, rain)

8 (well, work, pail)   (shop, cut, know)

9 (foot, glove, hand)   (knee, head, shake)

10 (under, over, through)   (sky, place, water)   5

Fill in the crosswords so that all the given words are included. You have been given one letter as a clue in each crossword.

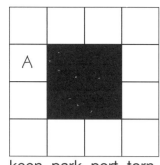

11

12

keen, park, port, torn   easy, heal, hole, lazy

2

Underline one word in the brackets which is most opposite in meaning to the word in capitals.

    Example   WIDE (broad   vague   long   <u>narrow</u>   motorway)

13 HEALTHY   (good   doctor   hospital   ill   patient)

14 TEACHER   (school   pupil   lesson   term   tutor)

15 FRIEND   (pal   mate   foe   ally   neighbour)

16 MANY   (more   lots   few   crowd   half)

17 WHOLE   (entire   part   some   complete   full)

5

Find the three-letter word which can be added to the letters in capitals to make a new word. The new word will complete the sentence sensibly.

    Example   The cat sprang onto the MO.   USE

18 A baby is an INT.   _____

19 A baby goes out in a P.   _____

20 A baby CLS on the floor.   _____

21 A baby plays with a TLE.   _____

22 A baby sits in a HIGHCH.   _____

5

Add one letter to the word in capital letters to make a new word. The meaning of the new word is given in the clue.

Example PLAN simple *plain*

23 WAS an insect _____

24 HOP to expect the best _____

25 LOW the opposite of fast _____

26 HAT to stop _____

27 RAN it pours _____

5

Complete the following expressions by underlining the missing word.

Example Frog is to tadpole as swan is to (duckling, baby, cygnet).

28 Sun is to sunk as pin is to (sink, pin, pink).

29 Eye is to see as ear is to (speak, hear, nose).

30 Bed is to bead as led is to (late, lead, deal).

31 Top is to bottom as right is to (correct, under, left).

32 Speak is to talk as consider is to (count, think, moan).

33 Ail is to bail as ill is to (sill, will, bill).

6

34   boy   but   why   she   sty

If these words were written backwards, which word would now come first in alphabetical order?

_____

1

These words have been written in code, but the codes are not under the right words.

BE	BEG	BIN	BEGIN	BEE
244	24538	24	245	238

Write the correct code for each word.

35 BE   36 BEG   37 BIN   38 BEE   39 BEGIN

_____   _____   _____   _____   _____

5

12

If a = 3, b = 2, d = 6, e = 8, f = 10, find the value of:

40 2f − 2a = __

41 2e − 2b = __

Sue and Omar wear yellow tops.

Lee and Omar wear green trousers.

Sue and Jess wear brown trousers.

Jess and Lee wear red tops.

Who wears:

42 a yellow top and brown trousers? _____

43 a red top and green trousers? _____

44 a yellow top and green trousers? _____

45 a red top and brown trousers? _____

Now go to the Progress Chart to record your score! Total 45

Paper 5

Which one letter can be added to the front of all of these words to make new words.

Example <u>c</u>are <u>c</u>at <u>c</u>rate <u>c</u>all

1 __arm __and __as __ollow

2 __old __hill __loud __an

3 __read __ream __ark __ome

4 __and __right __ear __each

5 __rim __ower __ride __lant

The train was due in at 10:50. It was 10 minutes late.

6 When did it arrive? _____

I left home at 18:15. It took me 20 minutes to walk to the cinema.

7 When did I get there? _____

A pudding takes 50 minutes to cook. I want it to be ready for 13:00.

8 When must I put it into the oven? _____   3

If these words were placed in alphabetical order, which word would come first?

9 Monday   Thursday   Wednesday   Friday   Tuesday   _____

10 May   January   March   February   April   _____

11 giraffe   elephant   mouse   horse   dog   _____

12 plane   helicopter   kite   balloon   rocket   _____   4

Underline one word in the brackets which is most opposite in meaning to the word in capitals.

Example   WIDE   (broad   vague   long   <u>narrow</u>   motorway)

13 WARM   (hot   cold   icy   sun   fine)

14 BLACK   (dark   brown   white   sooty   coal)

15 HIDE   (lost   last   find   secret   conceal)

16 MORE   (less   many   few   lots   plenty)

17 FIRST   (top   bottom   side   last   enough)   5

Underline two words which are made from the same letters.

Example   TAP   PET   <u>TEA</u>   POT   <u>EAT</u>

18 MAUL   PART   MAKE   TRAM   TRAP

19 AGES   ALES   APES   SAGE   SAND

20 LIMP   LEAP   PEEP   PEAL   PEARL

21 WARN   WARM   WARD   WARP   DRAW

22 LATE   LINT   TALE   TILE   FILE   5

Remove one letter from the word in capitals to leave a new word. The meaning of the new word is given in the clue.

Example AUNT an insect ant

23 ROAD   a stick   _____

24 PINT   something we use when sewing   _____

25 TINT   a metal   _____

26 CODE   a type of fish   _____

27 HARM   part of our body   _____   5

Underline the number that completes each sequence.

28 4 is to 16 as 16 is to (72, 64, 60)

29 3 is to 12 as 12 is to (24, 36, 48)

30 32 is to 16 as 16 is to (4, 8, 12)

31 55 is to 11 as 60 is to (11, 12, 14)

32 100 is to 50 as 90 is to (55, 40, 45)   5

These words have been written in code, but the codes are not under the right words.

STOW	SLOW	STEW	LOW	STOLE
9687	96418	9147	9647	147

Write the correct code for each word.

33 STOW   34 SLOW   35 STEW   36 LOW   37 STOLE

_____   _____   _____   _____   _____   5

Underline the word in the brackets which goes best with the words given outside the brackets.

Example word, paragraph, sentence (pen, cap, letter, top, stop)

38 bed, bunk, mattress   (drawer, cold, warm, film, pillow)

39 car, lorry, bicycle   (train, road, bus, speed, track)

40 sheep, cows, chickens   (farm, tractor, shed, pigs, bird)

41 money, cash, notes	(cheque, bank, lesson, coins, save)
42 mat, tiles, carpet	(curtains, rug, kitchen, sofa, stairs)

Fill in the crosswords so that all the given words are included. You have been given one letter as a clue in each crossword.

43

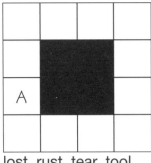

lost, rust, tear, tool

44

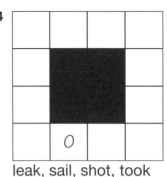

leak, sail, shot, took

45

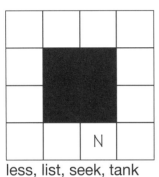

less, list, seek, tank

Now go to the Progress Chart to record your score! Total 45

Paper 6

Underline one word in the brackets which is most opposite in meaning to the word in capital letters.

Example WIDE (broad vague long <u>narrow</u> motorway)

1 SHORT (length long low metre up)

2 UP (saw went go down tall)

3 YOUNG (old clothes pretty dress new)

4 EVEN (smooth plain old odd straight)

5 FASTEN (collar fix loosen tie bind)

Fill in the crosswords so that all the given words are included. You have been given one letter as a clue in each crossword.

6

	R		
	■	■	
	■	■	

even, idle, iron, noon

7

	E		
	■		
		■	
	■		

told, nail, want, went

8

		T	
	■		
	■		

bare, hare, bath, rear

○ 3

In each line one word has been muddled up. Rearrange the letters so it fits in with the others.

Example fly spider moth gnat <u>tan</u>   <u>ant</u>

9 dove lark   wren   tit   low   _____

10 rain   owns mist   hail   fog   _____

11 lump pear date lime apple   _____

12 cake pork wets buns ham   _____

13 goat lamb deer loaf calf   _____

○ 5

Change the first word into the last word by changing one letter at a time and making a new, different word in the middle.

Example   CASE <u>CASH</u> LASH

14 LAND   _____   PAID

15 PLAN   _____   CLAP

16 PAID   _____   HAIL

(17)

17 WAND _____ FIND

18 SILK _____ TILL

5

Change the first word of the third pair in the same way as the other pairs to give a new word.

Example bind, hind   bare, hare   but, <u>hut</u>

19 rest, test   road, toad   rent, _____

20 chip, hip   park, ark   mice, _____

21 tear, tar   fear, far   bear, _____

22 bet, beat   set, seat   met, _____

23 and, band   old, bold   all, _____

5

In each line, underline the word that has its letters in alphabetical order.

24 ace   debt   eight   more

25 few   lips   most   room

2

Find the three-letter word which can be added to the letters in capitals to make a new word. The new word will complete the sentence sensibly.

Example The cat sprang onto the MO.   <u>USE</u>

26 A donkey BS. _____

27 A cock CS. _____

28 A lion RS. _____

29 A dog BS. _____

30 A pig GTS. _____

5

If the code for LATHER is ABCDEF, what are the codes for the following words?

31 REAL _____   **32** LATE _____   **33** HEAL _____

What do these codes stand for?

34 DEF _____   **35** CEECD _____

5

The day after tomorrow is Friday.

36 What was the day before yesterday? _____

If Joshua was a year older he would be three times as old as his brother. His brother is 4.

37 How old is Joshua? _____

I have 20p more than Gita who has 40p less than Mike. Mike has £1.20.

38 How much does Gita have? _____

39 How much do I have? _____

4

Underline the two words which are the odd ones out in the following groups of words.

Example black   king   purple   green   house

40 banana   pear   yellow   purple   apple

41 finger   ring   knee   hat   ear

42 rose   daffodil   daisy   leaf   stem

43 tennis   bat   ball   rugby   swimming

4

Fill in the crosswords so that all the given words are included. You have been given one letter as a clue in each crossword.

44
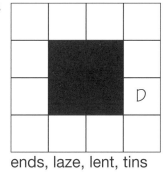
ends, laze, lent, tins

45
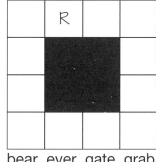
bear, ever, gate, grab

2

Paper 7

Look at these groups of words.

Group A Animals   Group B Colours   Group C Birds

Choose the correct group for each of the words below. Write in the letter.

1 purple ___   **2** ferret ___   **3** swan ___   **4** rabbit ___   **5** wren ___   5

Underline the pair of words most opposite in meaning.

	Example	cup, mug	coffee, milk	hot, cold
6	yes, no	tall, fat	roam, wander
7	happy, glad	teach, learn	blue, sea
8	sorry, cry	quick, run	less, more
9	work, play	high, jump	bright, shining
10	rain, puddle	cat, food	wet, dry

5

Underline the one word which **cannot be made** from the letters of the word in capital letters.

Example   STATIONERY   stone   tyres   ration   nation   noisy

11 PROFITS   frost   stiff   spot   soft   sport

12 GROWING   ring   gnaw   grin   wing   iron

13 COWARDS   ward   draws   soars   sword   crow

14 GRAPPLE   pear   rage   leap   gate   grape

15 PATIENT   tape   pint   teen   tent   neat

5

Look at the first group of three words. The word in the middle has been made from the other two words. Complete the second group of three words in the same way, making a new word in the middle.

Example   PAIN   INTO   TOOK   ALSO   SOON   ONLY

16 CAME   MESH   SHOT   YEAR   _____   CHIN

17 GRIN   GRAB   STAB   PLUM   _____   SCAN

18 MALT   ALSO   SAGO   SMOG   _____   SEAS

19 GATE   GAME   TIME   ROPE   _____   HOSE

20 THIN   MOTH   MOON   STAB   _____   PEGS

5

Complete the following sentences by selecting the most sensible word from each group of words given in the brackets. Underline the words selected.

Example   The (children, books, foxes) carried the (houses, books, steps) home from the (greengrocer, library, factory).

21 Tom saw a (bird, walrus, rabbit) run down a (chimney, hole, pavement) and into its (drey, burrow, sleep).

22 I feel (cold, lazy, hot) so I must put on a (swim suit, jumper, sandals) – then I will feel warmer in this chilly (sun, wind, day).

23 The (firework, balloons, streamers) were (burst, inflated, candle) to decorate the (room, table, ladder) for the party.

24 Clare (wrote, played, sent) a (page, text, letter) to Anya's mobile (bike, phone, pencil).

25 They (ran, walked, swam) across the (house, class, lake) to the (mist, frog, island).

5

Remove one letter from the word in capital letters to leave a new word. The meaning of the new word is given in the clue.

Example   AUNT   an insect   _ant_

26 BLESS   fewer   _____

27 THEN   a chicken   _____

28 MEAN   male   _____

29 REED   a colour   _____

4

Fill in the crosswords so that all the given words are included. You have been given one letter as a clue in each crossword.

30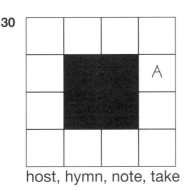

host, hymn, note, take

31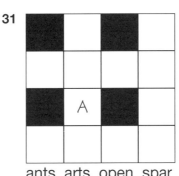

ants, arts, open, spar

2

32 If the code for SPIN is ABDE, what is the code for NIPS? _____

33 If the code for RING is CDEF, what is the code for GRIN? _____

34 If the code for SPRIG is ABCDF, what is the code for PRIG? _____

35 If the code for SEAT is 3521, what is the code for TEAS? _____

36 If the code for STEAM is 31526, what is the code for MAST? _____   ⬭ 5

Fill in the missing number or letters in each sequence.

Example   2   4   6   8   <u>10</u>

37 10   20   40   —   160

38 28   24   20   —   12

39 19   25   —   37   43

40 11   —   17   20   23

41 bb   bc   bd   —   bf   ⬭ 5

Look at this chart.

	English	Art	Maths	Science	ICT
Girls	5	6	2	1	3
Boys	4	2	4	6	3

42 Which subject is liked by twice as many boys as girls? _____

43 Which subject is three times as popular with girls as with boys? _____

44 Which subject is most popular with boys? _____

45 Which subject was liked equally well by boys and girls? _____   ⬭ 4

Now go to the Progress Chart to record your score!   Total ⬭ 45

Paper 8

If a = 1, b = 2, c = 3, d = 4, e = 5, f = 6, find the sum of:

1 a + b + c = __   **2** d + e + f = __

3 2a + b = __   **4** 2b + c = __

5 3a + 2b = __   **6** e + f = __   ⬭ 6

Rearrange the muddled letters in capitals to make a proper word. The answer will complete the sentence sensibly.

Example   A BEZAR is an animal with stripes.   <u>ZEBRA</u>

7   Half of six is HERET.   _____

8   Sheep have a thick OLWO coat.   _____

9   Don't drop TILTRE in the street.   _____

10   The fire crew used AETRW to put out the blaze.   _____

11   The tower of the HRCCHU was floodlit.   _____   ◯ 5

Complete the following sentences by selecting the most sensible word from each group of words given in the brackets. Underline the words selected.

Example   The (<u>children</u>, books, foxes) carried the (houses, <u>books</u>, steps) home from the (greengrocer, <u>library</u>, factory).

12   It was (hot, cold, freezing) and she (hated, wanted, disliked) a (pie, hot soup, cold drink) to cool her down.

13   Where is my (shoe, coat, book)? I left it (hiding, running, hanging) in the (shelf, kitchen, cupboard).

14   The (king, soldier, dog) sat in his (car, basket, larder) and (swam, growled, argued).   ◯ 3

Underline the pair of words most opposite in meaning.

Example   cup, mug   coffee, milk   <u>hot, cold</u>

15   cross, happy   sad, sorry   start, begin

16   neat, tidy   hard, soft   soap, water

17   eat, drink   boil, water   loud, noisy

18   cold, cool   shut, open   oil, tank

19   paper, pencil   pen, write   cry, laugh   ◯ 5

Look at the first group of three words. The word in the middle has been made from the other two words. Complete the second group of three words in the same way, making a new word in the middle.

Example   PAIN   INT<u>O</u>   T<u>OO</u>K   ALSO   <u>SOON</u>   ONLY

20   RASH   RAIN   GRIN   CLAN   _____   SLIP

21   POST   STAR   ARMY   POSH   _____   INTO

22	CRAG	CREW	EWES	BLUE	_____	ABLE
23	CHAT	CHIN	RAIN	SLAT	_____	SHAM
24	OVEN	VERY	YOUR	BACK	_____	ETCH

5

Underline the two words which are the odd ones out in the following groups of words.

Example black <u>king</u> purple green <u>house</u>

25	cot	sleep	cradle	sing	bed
26	cat	little	water	minute	small
27	road	long	tall	street	fat
28	coat	new	dress	pretty	suit
29	sorry	pleased	happy	glad	old

5

Fill in the missing letters. The alphabet has been written out to help you.

A B C D E F G H I J K L M N O P Q R S T U V W X Y Z

Example AB is to CD as PQ is to <u>RS</u>.

30 A30 is to B29 as C28 is to _____.

31 D20 is to E19 as F18 is to _____.

32 100A is to 95B as 90C is to _____.

33 A2 is to B3 as C4 is to _____.

34 F1 is to E2 as D3 is to _____.

5

Find and underline the two words which need to change places for each sentence to make sense.

Example She went to <u>letter</u> the <u>write</u>.

35 The drive was parked in the car.

36 We went to holiday for our Scotland.

37 I have to eat my pudding before I can have supper.

38 The shop on my road sweets sells.

39 We are moving our house and selling to Wales.

5

24

If the code for SECOND is ABCDEF, what are the codes for the following words?

40 ONE _____   41 CODE _____   42 ONCE _____

What do these codes stand for?

43 FDEB _____   44 FDAB _____   45 ABEF _____

Now go to the Progress Chart to record your score!   Total ◯ 45

6

Paper 9

Underline the pair of words most similar in meaning.

Example   come, go   <u>roam, wander</u>   fear, fare

1 fade, tint   blank, empty   hinder, go

2 cut, slit   hit, miss   less, more

3 dry, fine   rich, poor   tea, coffee

4 add, subtract   hole, gap   red, colour

5 tired, weary   hot, cold   forgot, remember

5

Find the three-letter word which can be added to the letters in capitals to make a new word. The new word will complete the sentence sensibly.

Example   The cat sprang onto the MO.   <u>USE</u>

6 The police will FOL the criminal.   _____

7 A DON is sometimes called an ass.   _____

8 Time to stop for a DR of water.   _____

9 He was pleased to go home from HOSAL.   _____

10 You need a BET to carry your shopping in.   _____

5

Find the letter which will end the first word and start the second word.

Example   peac (<u>h</u>) ome

11 gat (__) nds   12 non (__) ars   13 min (__) ust

14 ben (__) rim   15 als (__) dds

5

25

Look at the first group of three words. The word in the middle has been made from the other two words. Complete the second group of three words in the same way, making a new word in the middle.

Example   PAIN   INTO   TOOK   ALSO   SOON   ONLY

16 CLAN   CLOP   STOP   RATS   _____   FISH

17 BAND   BARK   DARK   SLIP   _____   GROW

18 FISH   SHOE   WOES   FAST   _____   TOWN

19 SALT   ALSO   SOOT   PART   _____   CHOP

20 BUSH   BUNK   PINK   STEP   _____   SHOP   ◯ 5

Complete the following sentences by selecting the most sensible word from each group of words given in the brackets. Underline the words selected.

Example   The (children, books, foxes) carried the (houses, books, steps) home from the (greengrocer, library, factory).

21 She spent a (lot, little, some) of money on all the things she had to (buy, sell, gather) for the big (party, card, mess).

22 The (dog, cow, rabbit) barked (kindly, fiercely, slowly) at the (burglars, robbing, scare).

23 Tola (buy, bought, bring) her brother a DVD as a (present, surprised, gifts) for (his, her, my) birthday.

24 Don't (run, walk, stand)! You'll (stop, wait, trip) and hurt your (book, friend, knee).

25 The cinema was (dry, packed, fill) for the premiere of the (pictures, movie, showing) with an all-star (sky, moon, cast).   ◯ 5

If the code for WONDER is 324165, what are the codes for the following words?

26 END _____   27 DEW _____

What do these codes stand for?

28 324 _____   29 3564 _____   30 246 _____   ◯ 5

If a = 1, b = 2, c = 3, d = 4, e = 5, find the sum of:

31 c + d + b = __   32 2a + 2 = __   33 2c + 2d = __   ◯ 3

It takes 1 hour 30 minutes to do the journey. Fill in the missing times.

34–37

Southby (depart)	Eastby (arrive)
_____	12:00
14:30	_____
16:10	_____
_____	18:30

4

If the letters in the following words are arranged in alphabetical order, which letter comes in the middle?

38 FAIRY _____

39 PLACE _____

40 LIGHT _____

41 TEACH _____

4

Worzles and Dingbats like to eat leaves and shoots.

Sninks and Dingbats like snails and slugs.

Worzles and Wigglers like weeds and grass.

Wigglers and Sninks like flies and berries.

42 Who likes berries but not weeds? _____

43 Who likes leaves, shoots and slugs? _____

44 Who likes snails and flies? _____

45 Who likes weeds, grass, flies and berries? _____

4

Now go to the Progress Chart to record your score! Total 45

Paper 10

Underline the two words which are the odd ones out in the following groups of words.

Example black <u>king</u> purple green <u>house</u>

1 child wash clean parent bath

2 circle newspaper ring hoop comic

3	grey	yellow	apple	blue	cherry
4	jeans	turban	white	brown	sweater
5	bench	arm	seat	chair	leg

⬭ 5

Find the three-letter word which can be added to the letters in capitals to make a new word. The new word will complete the sentence sensibly.

Example The cat sprang onto the MO. <u>USE</u>

6 The CH he sat on was hard. _____

7 The CSE of the river was long and winding. _____

8 The show INS at eight o'clock. _____

9 At the start of the play the ORS appeared on the stage. _____

10 The BN and white dog ran wildly after the ball. _____

⬭ 5

Find the letter which will end the first word and start the second word.

Example peac (h) ome

11 lan (—) are   12 fea (—) ule

13 gon (—) ver   14 sto (—) ond

15 cla (—) hite

⬭ 5

These words have been written in code, but the codes are not under the right words.

	AT	THE	CHAT	HAT	ACT
	2315	15	125	534	315

Write the correct code for each word.

16 AT   17 THE   18 CHAT

_____   _____   _____

19 HAT   20 ACT

_____   _____

⬭ 5

(28)

1 alley, lane
2 heavy, weighty
3 bite, nip
4 correct, right
5 closed, shut
6 EVE
7 HOE
8 ILL
9 HOW
10 FOR
11 below
12 inside
13 forgot
14 fingertip
15 handsome
16 pant
17 tear
18 tried
19 pain
20 stab
21 J
22 6H
23 DEG
24 PDE
25 6GH

26

H	O	M	E
I	▮	▮	D
N	▮	▮	I
T	E	N	T

27

T	E	R	M
I	▮	▮	O
M	▮	▮	S
E	N	D	S

28

W	I	S	H
A	▮	▮	E
G	▮	▮	A
S	H	I	P

29 18
30 2000
31 8
32 6.5
33 20
34 6
35 573
36 751
37 915
38 933
39 135
40 SPEAR
41 APPEAR
42 15 minutes
43 75 minutes
44 30 minutes
45 30 minutes

1 bright
2 fast
3 chuckle
4 new
5 easy
6 7
7 12
8 10
9 4
10 4
11 d
12 e
13 t
14 k
15 t

16

C	A	M	P
A	▮	▮	L
T	▮	▮	U
S	H	A	M

17

B	E	N	D
E	▮	▮	A
A	▮	▮	R
M	I	L	K

18

B	A	N	K
E	▮	▮	I
A	▮	▮	N
R	I	N	G

19 bedside
20 underground
21 inform
22 outlaw
23 forgive
24 PINE
25 COME
26 COPE
27 MATE
28 GOLD
29 5632
30 586
31 TOP
32 TOSS
33 ERR
34 walls
35 water
35 buildings
37 a stove
38 students
39 MEAT, TEAM
40 TEN, NET
41 LAST, SALT
42 far
43 ham
44 round
45 tan

1 crowd, concert
2 enlarge, expand
3 harbour, pier
4 weak, ill
5 swim, dive
6 ARM
7 EAR
8 JAM
9 COT
10 TEN
11 p
12 b
13 s
14 m
15 s
16 trout
17 noise
18 thick
19 plate
20 sport

21

M	I	S	T
A	■	■	R
R	■	■	I
K	E	E	P

22

H	A	L	F
A	■	■	I
R	■	■	R
D	A	T	E

23

P	A	R	T
E	■	■	I
A	■	■	D
R	I	P	E

24 12
25 6
26 36
27 54
28 343
29 722
30 247
31 727
32 72
33 46
34 6
35 7
36 6
37 dear
38 flow
39 eaten
40 need
41 got
42 ant
43 cry
44 dint
45 flow

Paper 4

1 tail, dog
2 sister, mother
3 bed, book
4 cake, party
5 office, bus
6 seaweed
7 sandcastle
8 workshop
9 handshake
10 underwater

11

P	O	R	T
A	■	■	O
R	■	■	R
K	E	E	N

12

H	E	A	L
O	■	■	A
L	■	■	Z
E	A	S	Y

13 ill
14 pupil
15 foe
16 few
17 part
18 FAN
19 RAM
20 RAW
21 RAT
22 AIR
23 wasp
24 hope
25 slow
26 halt
27 rain
28 pink
29 hear
30 lead
31 left
32 think
33 bill
34 she
35 24
36 245
37 238
38 244
39 24538
40 14
41 12
42 Sue
43 Lee
44 Omar
45 Jess

Paper 5

1 h
2 c
3 d
4 b
5 p
6 11:00
7 18:35
8 12:10
9 Friday
10 April
11 dog
12 balloon
13 cold
14 white
15 find
16 less
17 last
18 PART, TRAP
19 AGES, SAGE
20 LEAP, PEAL
21 WARD, DRAW
22 LATE, TALE
23 rod
24 pin
25 tin
26 cod
27 arm
28 64
29 48
30 8
31 12
32 45
33 9647
34 9147
35 9687
36 147
37 96418
38 pillow
39 bus
40 pigs
41 coins
42 rug
43

T	O	O	L
E	■	■	O
A	■	■	S
R	U	S	T

44

S	A	I	L
H	■	E	A
O	■	A	
T	O	O	K

45

L	E	S	S
I	■	E	
S	■	E	
T	A	N	K

Paper 6

1 long
2 down
3 old
4 odd
5 loosen
6

I	R	O	N
D	■	O	
L	■	O	
E	V	E	N

7

W	E	N	T
A	■	O	
N	A	I	L
T	■	D	

8

B	A	T	H
A	■	A	
R	E	A	R
E	■	E	

9 owl
10 snow
11 plum
12 stew
13 foal
14 LAID
15 CLAN
16 PAIL
17 WIND
18 SILL
19 tent
20 ice
21 bar
22 meat
23 ball

---

24 ace
25 most
26 RAY
27 ROW
28 OAR
29 ARK
30 RUN
31 FEBA
32 ABCE
33 DEBA
34 HER
35 TEETH
36 Monday
37 11
38 80p
39 £1.00
40 yellow, purple
41 ring, hat
42 leaf, stem
43 bat, ball
44

L	A	Z	E
E	■	■	N
N	■	■	D
T	I	N	S

45

G	R	A	B
A	■	■	E
T	■	■	A
E	V	E	R

Paper 7

1 B
2 A
3 C
4 A
5 C
6 yes, no
7 teach, learn
8 less, more
9 work, play
10 wet, dry
11 stiff
12 gnaw
13 soars
14 gate

---

15 teen
16 ARCH
17 PLAN
18 MOSS
19 ROSE
20 PEST
21 rabbit, hole, burrow
22 cold, jumper, wind
23 balloons, inflated, room
24 sent, text, phone
25 swam, lake, island
26 less
27 hen
28 man
29 red
30

H	O	S	T
Y	■	■	A
M	■	■	K
N	O	T	E

31

	S		A
■	S	■	A
O	P	E	N
■	A	■	T
A	R	T	S

32 EDBA
33 FCDE
34 BCDF
35 1523
36 6231
37 80
38 16
39 31
40 14
41 be
42 Maths
43 Art
44 Science
45 ICT

Paper 8

1 6
2 15
3 4
4 7
5 7
6 11

7 THREE
8 WOOL
9 LITTER
10 WATER
11 CHURCH
12 hot, wanted, cold drink
13 coat, hanging, cupboard
14 dog, basket, growled
15 cross, happy
16 hard, soft
17 eat, drink
18 shut, open
19 cry, laugh
20 CLIP
21 SHIN
22 BLAB
23 SLAM
24 ACHE
25 sleep, sing
26 cat, water
27 road, street
28 new, pretty
29 sorry, old
30 D27
31 G17
32 85D
33 D5
34 C4
35 drive, car
36 holiday, Scotland
37 pudding, supper
38 sweets, sells
39 moving, selling
40 DEB
41 CDFB
42 DECB
43 DONE
44 DOSE
45 SEND

6 LOW
7 KEY
8 INK
9 PIT
10 ASK
11 e
12 e
13 d
14 t
15 o
16 RASH
17 SLOW
18 STOW
19 ARCH
20 STOP
21 lot, buy, party
22 dog, fiercely, burglars
23 bought, present, his
24 run, trip, knee
25 packed, movie, cast
26 641
27 163
28 WON
29 WREN
30 ONE
31 9
32 4
33 14
34–37 Southby depart 10:30
      Eastby arrive 16:00
      Eastby arrive 17:40
      Southby depart 17:00
38 I
39 E
40 I
41 E
42 Sninks
43 Dingbats
44 Sninks
45 Wigglers

6 AIR
7 OUR
8 BEG
9 ACT
10 ROW
11 d
12 r
13 e
14 p
15 w
16 15
17 534
18 2315
19 315
20 125
21 fork
22 E
23 spade, beach, castle
24 fixed, pipe, basin
25 heard, burglar, house
26 help, lift, table
27 owl, hooted, wood
28 w
29 b
30 f
31 o
32 c
33 SORT
34 BULK
35 STAB
36 HOPE
37 EASY
38 loud
39 cub
40 shin
41 lie
42 pan
43 tools, stool
44 slip, lips
45 toga, goat

Paper 9

1 blank, empty
2 cut, slit
3 dry, fine
4 hole, gap
5 tired, weary

Paper 10

1 child, parent
2 newspaper, comic
3 apple, cherry
4 white, brown
5 arm, leg

Paper 11

1

2

	H		N	
T	A	M	E	
		T	E	
U	S	E	D	

3

C	A	F	E
A		I	
R	U	S	H
T		H	

4 yawned, tired, bed
5 bike, swerved, road
6 climbed, window, castle
7 turned, lights, dark
8 danced, rhythm, music
9 <u>hairdresser</u>, dentist
10 <u>cage</u>, pool
11 <u>newspaper</u>, dictionary
12 <u>rice</u>, bread
13 <u>candle</u>, cake
14 KEGCK
15 KGCE
16 ACI
17 IGCK
18 TRAP
19 REAP
20 PART
21 mist
22 all
23 rake
24 boat
25 burden, load
26 kind, thoughtful
27 expect, hope
28 little, small
29 hide, conceal
30 SHE
31 RAN
32 KIN
33 AGE
34 HIT
35 e
36 h
37 k
38 e
39 e
40 in
41 be

42 sea
43 out
44 sand
45 air

Paper 12

1–5 Give one mark for each two right answers:
cricket C, peas D, axe A, drum B, saw A, guitar B, potatoes D, hammer A, piano B, football C
6 w
7 s
8 w
9 t
10 f
11 outfit
12 beside
13 farewell
14 afterwards
15 checkout
16 boy
17 doctors
18 calf
19 sheep
20 burrow

21

S		S	
N	E	W	S
A		A	
G	O	N	E

22

	R		A
H	E	L	D
	A		D
A	P	E	S

23

C	A	S	T
H		H	
E	V	E	N
W		D	

24 G
25 21
26 February
27 December
28 @ ÷ +

29 × ÷ @
30 − ÷ ×
31 WAR
32 STAR
33 Mr Young's age: 30
34 Joshua's age: 2
35 Joshua's age:10
36 race, teacher, whistle
37 birds, seed, garden
38 flowers, pot, door
39 table, forks, knives
40 cars, work, morning
41 outside, cold
42 apple, salad
43 holiday, Christmas
44 road, car
45 moon, window

Paper 13

1

S		C	
P	E	A	S
I		L	
T	I	M	E

2

	T		H
T	A	L	E
	I		R
A	L	S	O

3

G	I	R	L
A		U	
T	I	D	Y
E		E	

4 unhappy, sad
5 sharp, pointed
6 loud, noisy
7 cheap, inexpensive
8 terror, fear
9 sad
10 starve
11 still
12 dirty
13 hinder
14 O
15 N
16 E
17 F

18 rear
19 sore
20 late
21 tale
22 sing
23 ride
24 6413
25 1563
26 463
27 NOON
28 SOON
29 28
30 34
31 19
32 fear
33 need
34 rote
35 none
36 star
37 hair
38 under
39 ship
40 up
41 cart
42 1
43 3
44 2
45 4

Paper 14

1 PINK
2 GREY
3 NAVY
4 MAUVE
5 BROWN
6 hotplate
7 rainbow
8 toothache
9 football
10 fireplace
11 moist
12 flower
13 front
14 trots
15 ground
16 go, come

17 night, day
18 full, empty
19 tall, short
20 play, work
21
22
23
24 CG
25 8H
26 WE
27 4S
28 JP
29 ÷ % − +
30 + % ÷
31 × % ÷
32 MAST
33 ARMS
34 d
35 g
36 b
37 none
38 Annie
39 Kim
40 Thursday
41 tired, exhausted
42 swerve, dodge
43 mean, stingy
44 soldiers, troops
45 double, twice

Paper 15

1 grass, lawn
2 wash, dry
3 house, cottage
4 plate, dish
5 glove, hat
6 light
7 wing
8 cure
9 cat
10 hat
11
12
13
14 sip
15 feat
16 wets
17 race
18 flat
19 6
20 7
21 12
22 birthday, mother, cake
23 eat, chips, fish
24 night, wet, windy
25 eat, cake, poisoned
26 people, seen, city
27 + − − +
28 ÷ / × −
29 − + × ÷ − /
30 ONION
31 TINT
32 hold
33 final
34 rich
35 stake
36 near, far
37 save, spend
38 ugly, pretty
39 friend, enemy
40 quiet, noisy

41 year, sea
42 school, house
43 had, I
44 ways, both
45 seeds, flowers

41 feed
42 face
43 bead
44 fade
45 add

41 seed
42 icy
43 slide
44 lift
45 tilt

Paper 16

1 tired, she, sit
2 sister, dance, boyfriend
3 left, purse, shop
4 ring, ambulance, mobile
5 supper, moon, sky
6 trees
7 a tail
8 man
9 with patients
10 roots
11 December
12 eleven
13 individual
14 release
15 alabaster
16 $+ - \times \div /$
17 $\div + + - \times$
18 $+ \div - \times$
19 DALE
20 DEED
21 crate
22 sold
23 hole
24 hard
25 super
26 children
27 pens
28 noises
29 bungalow
30 box
31 beginning, end
32 open, closed
33 high, low
34 strong, weak
35 quiet, loud
36 END
37 NUT
38 ODE
39 EAR
40 WAR

Paper 17

1 10
2 11
3 11
4 8
5 3
6 heavy, light
7 here, there
8 whisper, shout
9 late, early
10 glad, sad
11 ACE
12 ROT
13 TON
14 ROW
15 JOY
16 d
17 e
18 t
19 k
20 t
21 NEST
22 CHIN
23 BASH
24 BEAT
25 BEST
26 help, aid
27 ruin, spoil
28 angry, cross
29 hear, listen
30 price, cost
31 5
32 9
33 4
34 8
35 3
36 49
37 30
38 28
39 250
40 76

Paper 18

1–5 Give one mark for each two correct answers: whisk A, camel D, Dutch B, scales A, gull C, German B, lamb D, recipe A, goose C, French B
6 ATE
7 CAR
8 ARE
9 WAS
10 TEA
11 d
12 t
13 g
14 p
15 e
16

E		S	
Y	E	L	L
E		O	
S	I	P	S

17

F	O	O	D
L		A	
A	C	T	S
G		S	

18 seat
19 list
20 moat
21 heat
22 than
23 $- / \times$
24 $\$ = / @ \times$
25 $= / @ + /$
26 TAG
27 GATE
28 B
29 D
30 A

ANSWERS

Bond Verbal Reasoning Assessment Papers 8–9 years

31 C
32 bead
33 E
34 K
35 S
36 words, spelling, school
37 writer, study, book
38 landed, broke, applause
39 sister, boyfriend, birthday
40 spent, weekend, lines
41 leave, depart
42 bitter, sour
43 calm, peaceful
44 sweep, brush
45 grateful, thankful

Paper 19

1 same
2 say
3 let
4 beloved
5 tree
6 OUR
7 RAN
8 BAN
9 HAD
10 PEN
11 e
12 t
13 e
14 t
15 o
16 MV
17 8H
18 ABD
19 Nb
20 7VU
21

22

23

24 CASTLE
25 ANYONE
26 PIRATE
27 CINEMA
28 SHOPPING
29 145
30 541
31 144
32 146
33 6417
34 queen, castle, crown
35 clock, on time school
36 winter, snow, sledging
37 ill, medicine, better
38 nap
39 send
40 poke
41 soil
42 aunt
43 16
44 18
45 28

Paper 20

1 D50
2 35D
3 DW
4 GH
5 T
6 11
7 32
8 20
9 18

10 35
11 425
12 266
13 4275
14 4751
15 256
16 26
17 13
18 16
19 INCH, CHIN
20 BRUSH, SHRUB
21 NEAR, EARN
22 CLASP, SCALP
23 feet, teeth
24 pig, dog
25 reason, fault
26 brief, short
27 glad, happy
28 yell, scream
29 talk, speak
30 see, look
31 BAT
32 HIP
33 OAR
34 LOW
35 RED
36 l
37 t
38 d
39 t
40 e
41 helpless
42 setback
43 matchstick
44 message
45 indoors

21 four   fork   fire   fall   feel

If these words were placed in alphabetical order, which word would come fourth?

_____

22 If the letters in the following word are arranged in alphabetical order, which letter comes in the middle?

CHASE _____   **2**

Complete the following sentences by selecting the most sensible word from each group of words given in the brackets. Underline the words selected.

> **Example** The (children, books, foxes) carried the (houses, books, steps) home from the (greengrocer, library, factory).

23 Mai took her (spoon, spade, hoe) to the (garden, beach, park) to build a (bridge, castle, palace).

24 The workman (knocked, fixed, tied) the (string, pipe, paper) to the (basin, cooker, table) in the bathroom.

25 No one (heard, wanted, bought) the (washing, burglar, road) enter the (kennel, fridge, house).

26 Can you (wait, hinder, help) me (empty, lift, buy) this box onto the (lawn, table, dog)?

27 The (monster, policeman, owl) (hooted, whispered, sang) in the (cupboard, hall, wood).   **5**

Which one letter can be added to the front of all these words to make new words?

> **Example**   care   cat   crate   call

28 __hale   __rap   __in   __art

29 __lame   __right   __one   __urn

30 __lint   __ray   __rank   __lea

31 __pen   __at   __pal   __range

32 __lip   __limb   __heat   __harm   **5**

Look at the first group of three words. The word in the middle has been made from the other two words. Complete the second group of three words in the same way, making a new word in the middle of the group.

Example PAIN INTO TOOK   ALSO <u>SOON</u> ONLY

33 VEST   VEIN   PAIN   SOME   _____   TART

34 HARP   PART   PORT   GULP   _____   BARK

35 MASH   SHIP   TRIP   FIST   _____   GRAB

36 SELL   SEAT   BEAT   HOME   _____   RIPE

37 MARK   ARMS   HEMS   PEAL   _____   BUSY   ◯ 5

Remove one letter from the word in capital letters to leave a new word. The meaning of the new word is given in the clue.

Example AUNT   an insect   <u>ant</u>

38 CLOUD   not quiet   _____

39 CLUB   a baby bear   _____

40 SHINE   part of the leg   _____

41 LIFE   a fib   _____

42 PANT   used for cooking   _____   ◯ 5

43–45 In each list of words, the letters of one word have been jumbled up. Underline it and write it correctly.

FURNITURE   PARTS OF THE BODY   ANIMALS

   piano   slip   mare

   tools   nose   frog

   table   eyes   toga

   _____   _____   _____   ◯ 3

Paper 11

Fill in the crosswords so that all the given words are included. You have been given one letter as a clue in each crossword.

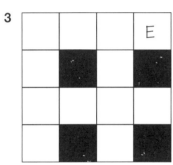

1   ever, done, opal, late

2   hats, need, tame, used

3   café, cart, fish, rush

Complete the following sentences by selecting the most sensible word from each group of words given in the brackets. Underline the words selected.

Example   The (<u>children</u>, books, foxes) carried the (houses, <u>books</u>, steps) home from the (greengrocer, <u>library</u>, factory).

4   The old lady (smiled, yawned, laughed) because she was (tired, worried, ill) and wanted to go to (hospital, bed, play).

5   The (bike, ship, bed) (fell, swerved, ran) across the (pond, road, door).

6   He carefully (waited, cooked, climbed) through the (roof, garden, window) into the (zoo, kennel, castle).

7   She (climbed, shouted, turned) on the (lights, curtains, towels) as it was getting (light, dark, sunny).

8   Alex (hum, danced, clap) to the (rhythm, rhyme, tone) of the (music, chair, spoon).

3

5

Change one word so that the sentence makes sense. Underline the word you are taking out and write your new word on the line.

Example   I waited in line to buy a <u>book</u> to see the film.   *ticket*

9 I had a toothache so my mother took me to the hairdresser. _____

10 The swimming cage in my town has two diving boards.   _____

11 When I asked my mum what a word meant she told me to
look it up in the newspaper.   _____

12 For lunch I like a cheese sandwich on brown rice and an
apple.   _____

13 My birthday candle this year is going to be chocolate sponge. _____   5

If the code for PARENT is ACEGIK, what are the codes for the following words?

14 TREAT _____   15 TEAR _____

16 PAN _____   17 NEAT _____

What do these codes stand for?

18 KECA _____   19 EGCA _____   20 ACEK _____   7

Change the first word of the third pair in the same way as the other pairs to give a new word.

Example   bind, hind   bare, hare   but, <u>hut</u>

21 light, might   line, mine   list, _____

22 hair, air   hand, and   ball, _____

23 beach, reach   best, rest   bake, _____

24 oil, boil   old, bold   oat, _____   4

Underline the pair of words most similar in meaning.

Example   come, go   <u>roam, wander</u>   fear, fare

25 help, hinder   hate, horrid   burden, load

26 kind, thoughtful   come, go   top, hill

27 low, slight   expect, hope   come, depart

28 little, small   fly, down   top, bottom

29 last, ever   one, once   hide, conceal   5

32

Find the three-letter word which can be added to the letters in capitals to make a new word. The new word will complete the sentence sensibly.

Example   The cat sprang onto the MO.   USE

30 We keep the mower in the garden D.   _____

31 The flowers are a bright OGE colour.   _____

32 She peeled the apple and composted the S.   _____

33 Some PS of the book were torn.   _____

34 I like the yolk but not the WE of egg.   _____   (5)

Find the letter which will end the first word and start the second word.

Example   peac (h) o m e

35 lon (__) ggs

36 bat (__) orn

37 mar (__) nit

38 pan (__) lse

39 mar (__) els   (5)

Find a word that can be put in front of each of the following words to make new, compound words.

Example   cast   fall   ward   pour   *down*

#					
40	side	crease	door	land	_____
41	cause	hind	neath	come	_____
42	side	shell	gull	bed	_____
43	side	standing	shine	right	_____
44	castle	pit	storm	paper	_____
45	port	bag	ship	craft	_____

(6)

Paper 12

1–5 Look at these groups of words.

Group A Tools   Group B Musical instruments
Group C Sports or games   Group D Vegetables

Choose the correct group for each of the words below. Write in the letter.

cricket __ peas __ axe __ drum __ saw __

guitar __ potatoes __ hammer __ piano __ football __

5

Find the letter which will end the first word and start the second word.

Example   peac (h) ome

6 blo (__) ish   **7** pas (__) pin   **8** sho (__) ind

9 mus (__) idy   **10** puf (__) eed

5

Underline two words, one from each group, that go together to form a new word. The word in the first group always comes first.

Example   (hand, green, for)   (light, house, sure)

11 (in, of, out)   (fit, ill, well)

12 (was, be, do)   (front, side, back)

13 (say, fare, end)   (ill, gone, well)

14 (before, when, after)   (come, wards, wet)

15 (check, pencil, pen)   (down, side, out)

5

Complete the following expressions by underlining the missing word.

Example   Frog is to tadpole as swan is to (duckling, baby, cygnet).

16 Aunt is to uncle as girl is to (boy, cousin, son).

17 Pupils are to teachers as patients are to (surgery, doctors, accident).

18 Dog is to puppy as cow is to (ram, lamb, calf).

19 Crowd is to people as flock is to (sheep, pigs, cows).

20 Pig is to sty as rabbit is to (drey, burrow, nest).

5

Fill in the crosswords so that all the given words are included. You have been given one letter as a clue in each crossword.

21

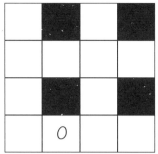

gone, news, snag, swan

22

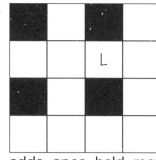

adds, apes, held, reap

23

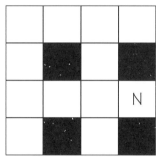

cast, chew, even, shed

◯ 3

24 If the first five letters of the alphabet were removed, which would be the second letter of those left? Circle the correct letter.

E H G F

25 How many letters would there be in this alphabet? Circle the correct number.

20 21 22

26 Which month of the year begins with the sixth letter of the usual alphabet? _____

27 Which month of the year begins with the fourth letter? _____

◯ 4

If the code for STRAW is $+ - \times \div @$, what are the codes for the following words?

28 WAS _____   **29** RAW _____   **30** TAR _____

What do these codes stand for?

31 $@ \div \times$ _____   **32** $+ - \div \times$ _____

◯ 5

33–35 Mr Young was 25 when Joshua was born. Complete the table.

Mr Young's age	27		35
Joshua's age		5	

3

Complete the following sentences by selecting the most sensible word from each group of words given in the brackets. Underline the words selected.

Example The (children, books, foxes) carried the (houses, books, steps) home from the (greengrocer, library, factory).

36 The (race, film, job) started when the (teacher, doctor, baker) blew her (crown, pencil, whistle).

37 My mum feeds the (birds, fish, cats) each morning by putting some (jam, seed, cake) out in the (car, bin, garden).

38 In our garden we have some (swings, rocks, flowers) in a (cup, pot, dish) that sit near the back (lake, road, door).

39 Jenny set the (chair, table, television) for supper by laying out the (books, pots, forks) and (pans, knives, apples).

40 The noise of the (bikes, trees, cars) as people go to (work, sleep, play) in the (morning, holiday, sun) wakes me.

5

Find and underline the two words which need to change places for each sentence to make sense.

Example She went to <u>letter</u> the <u>write</u>.

41 It is too outside to go cold today.

42 The fruit apple was made with grapes, pear and salad.

43 My aunt and uncle come and spend every holiday Christmas with us.

44 The police officer told the man to move his road because it was blocking the car.

45 Sometimes when I look out of my moon at night I can see the window.

5

Paper 13

Fill in the crosswords so that all the given words are included. You have been given one letter as a clue in each crossword.

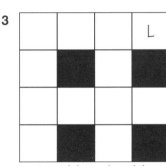

1

calm, peas, spit, time

2

R

also, hero, tail, tale

3

L

gate, girl, rude, tidy

Underline the pair of words most similar in meaning.

Example   come, go   <u>roam, wander</u>   fear, fare

4   unhappy, sad   many, few   speak, listen

5   accept, refuse   divide, add   sharp, pointed

6   buy, sell   throw, catch   loud, noisy

7   cheap, inexpensive   generous, mean   rough, smooth

8   feeble, strong   give, take   terror, fear

Underline one word in the brackets which is most opposite in meaning to the word in capitals.

Example   WIDE   (broad   vague   long   <u>narrow</u>   motorway)

9   CHEERFUL   (happy   pleased   sad   joyful   thoughtful)

10   EAT   (meals   starve   hungry   food   dine)

3

5

11 MOVING   (jump   still   run   skip   slow)

12 CLEAN   (tint   washed   dirty   dyed   spill)

13 HELP   (aid   assist   hinder   flop   earn)

5

If the letters in the following words are arranged in alphabetical order, which letter comes in the middle?

14 POUND   _____

15 TRAIN   _____

16 READS   _____

17 AFTER   _____

4

Remove one letter from the word in capital letters to leave a new word. The meaning of the new word is given in the clue.

Example   AUNT   an insect   <u>ant</u>

18 DREAR   at the back   _____

19 SHORE   painful   _____

20 PLATE   opposite of early   _____

21 STALE   a story   _____

22 SINGE   make a tune with the voice   _____

23 PRIDE   to go on horseback   _____

6

If the code for SEASON is 135146, what are the codes for the following words?

24 NOSE _____   25 SANE _____   26 ONE _____

What do these codes stand for?

27 6446 _____   28 1446 _____

5

The pegs on one side of a cloakroom are numbered 1 to 20. On the other side they are numbered 21 to 40. 1 is opposite 21.

29 What number peg is opposite 8?   __

30 What number peg is opposite 14?   __

31 What number peg is opposite 39?   __

3

Underline the one word which **cannot be made** from the letters of the word in capital letters.

Example   STATIONERY   stone   tyres   ration   <u>nation</u>   noisy

32 FLOWERS   slow   swore   fear   wore   flow

33 WANDER   wand   dear   draw   need   read

34 CURATE   rate   cater   rote   cart   care

35 MEANING   nine   main   game   none   mane

36 FASTEN   east   seat   neat   fate   star

(5

Find a word that can be put in front of each of the following words to make new, compound words.

Example   cast fall   ward   pour   *down*

37 pin   net   slide   dryer   ———

38 go   hand   mine   rate   ———

39 mate   yard   owner   shape   ———

40 roar   set   right   ward   ———

41 wheel   load   ridge   horse   ———

(5

Houses 1 and 2 have green doors.

Houses 2 and 3 have brown windows.

Houses 1 and 4 have blue windows.

Houses 4 and 3 have red doors.

Which house has:

42 a green door and blue windows?   ———

43 a red door and brown windows?   ———

44 a green door and brown windows?   ———

45 a red door and blue windows?   ———

(4

Paper 14

Rearrange the muddled letters in capitals to make proper words. They are all colours.

1 KPIN   _____   2 YREG   _____

3 YVAN   _____   4 AEUVM   _____

5 NORWB   _____

5

Underline two words, one from each group, that go together to form a new word. The word in the first group always comes first.

> **Example**   (hand, <u>green</u>, for)   (light, <u>house</u>, sure)

6 (old, hot, white)   (paper, plate, petal)

7 (rain, snow, wet)   (bow, arch, building)

8 (blood, tooth, pain)   (hurt, sore, ache)

9 (big, leg, foot)   (ball, park, shoe)

10 (fire, water, sea)   (switch, alarm, place)

5

Add one letter to the word in capital letters to make a new word. The meaning of the new word is given in the clue.

> **Example**   PLAN   simple   <u>plain</u>

11 MIST   to be damp   _____

12 LOWER   grows in the garden   _____

13 FONT   opposite of back   _____

14 ROTS   a horse does this   _____

15 ROUND   land   _____

5

Underline the two words, one from each group, which are the most opposite in meaning.

> **Exam**   (dawn, <u>early</u>, wake)   (<u>late</u>, stop, sunrise)

16 (go, back, front)   (here, for, come)

17 (moon, night, dark)   (day, shadow, dawn)

18 (full, small, big)   (over, tiny, empty)

19 (big, height, tall)   (large, short, huge)

20 (play, lazy, good)   (hard, cross, work)

Fill in the crosswords so that all the given words are included. You have been given one letter as a clue in each crossword.

21

asks, sago, seat, spot

22

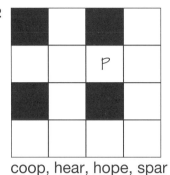

coop, hear, hope, spar

23

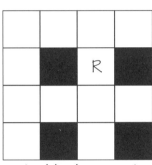

cart, chip, iron, root

Give the missing pairs of letters and numbers in the following sequences. The alphabet has been written out to help you.

A B C D E F G H I J K L M N O P Q R S T U V W X Y Z

	Example	CQ	DP	EQ	FP	_GQ_
24	AE	BF	—	DH	EI	
25	4D	5E	6F	7G	—	
26	ZB	YC	XD	—	VF	
27	2T	—	6R	8Q	10P	
28	—	KO	LN	MM	NL	

If the code for MASTER is + − × ÷ % @, what are the codes for the following words?

29 TEAM _____   **30** MET _____   **31** SET _____

What do these codes stand for?

32 $+ - \times \div$ _____

33 $- @ + \times$ _____

5

If a = 2, b = 3, c = 4, d = 5, e = 6, f = 7, g = 8, h = 9, find the sum of these questions. Give your answers as letters.

34 (g + f) ÷ b = _____   **35** a + (h − b) = _____   **36** ce ÷ g = _____

3

Some children do a paper round.

Mike does Wednesday and Saturday. He sometimes does Monday as well.

Sally does Monday and Thursday. She never helps on Saturday.

Annie does Monday and Wednesday. She sometimes helps on Thursday.

Kim does Thursday and Saturday. She sometimes helps on Wednesday.

37 How many of the children work on Tuesday?   _____

38 Who usually works on Wednesday but not Saturday?   _____

39 Who works on Thursday but not Monday?   _____

40 On which day of the week do Sally and Kim both work?

_____

4

Underline the pair of words most similar in meaning.

Example   come, go   <u>roam, wander</u>   fear, fare

41 unhappy, cross   tired, exhausted   run, skip

42 crawl, walk   sit, stand   swerve, dodge

43 mean, stingy   generous, poor   give, receive

44 army, navy   sea, harbour   soldiers, troops

45 first, last   first, tenth   double, twice

5

Now go to the Progress Chart to record your score!   Total   45

Paper 15

Underline the two words which are the odd ones out in the following groups of words.

> **Example**   black   <u>king</u>   purple   green   <u>house</u>

1   green   grass   blue   lawn   red

2   wash   friend   pal   dry   mate

3   cod   house   salmon   herring   cottage

4   plate   cheese   dish   bread   butter

5   shoe   glove   boot   hat   sandal

5

Remove one letter from the word in capital letters to leave a new word. The meaning of the new word is given in the clue.

> **Example**   AUNT   an insect   <u>ant</u>

6   FLIGHT   not heavy   _____

7   SWING   part of a bird   _____

8   CURVE   heal   _____

9   COAT   a pet   _____

10   HEAT   you wear it on your head   _____

5

Fill in the crosswords so that all the given words are included. You have been given one letter as a clue in each crossword.

11
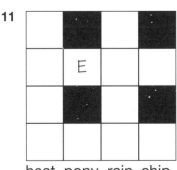
heat, pony, rain, ship

12
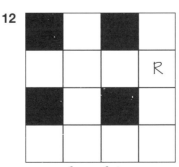
army, fear, fete, very

43

13

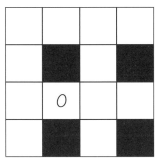

dote, late, wide, will

3

Change the first word of the third pair in the same way as the other pairs to give a new word.

Example   bind, hind   bare, hare   but, <u>hut</u>

14   crane, cane   plot, pot   ship, _____

15   pat, peat   wed, weed   fat, _____

16   rats, star   peek, keep   stew, _____

17   lime, mile   rite, tire   care, _____

18   sit, sat   clip, clap   flit, _____

5

If a = 1, b = 2, c = 3, d = 4, find the value of the following.

19   $a \times b \times c =$ __   20 $(b \times d) - a =$ __   21 $c \times d =$ __

3

Complete the following sentences by selecting the most sensible word from each group of words given in the brackets. Underline the words selected.

Example   The (<u>children</u>, books, foxes) carried the (houses, <u>books</u>, steps) home from the (greengrocer, <u>library</u>, factory).

22   On my (day, morning, birthday) my (dog, cat, mother) makes me a special (biscuit, cake, bun).

23   The girl liked to (sleep, climb, eat) (cereal, milk, chips) with her (table, soup, fish).

24   The (night, pond, moon) was (wet, slow, heavy) and (sunny, dry, windy).

25   Don't (burn, bake, eat) the (stone, king, cake). It's been (baked, poisoned, lost)!

26   Few (sheep, goats, people) have ever (seen, grazed, stolen) the ruined (hedge, pond, city).

5

If the code for POTION is $+ - \times \div - /$, what are the codes for the following words?

27 POOP _____   **28** INTO _____   **29** OPTION _____

What do these codes stand for?

30 $- / \div - /$ _____   **31** $\times \div / \times$ _____   ⑤

Underline the word in brackets closest in meaning to the word in capitals.

Example   UNHAPPY   (unkind   death   laughter   <u>sad</u>   friendly)

32 CONTAIN   (order   help   hold   drop   box)

33 LAST   (first   final   try   start   ending)

34 WEALTHY   (poor   money   banker   rich   cheque)

35 POST   (wood   stand   box   sign   stake)   ④

Underline the two words, one from each group, which are the most opposite in meaning.

Example   (dawn, <u>early</u>, wake)   (<u>late</u>, stop, sunrise)

36 (help, near, hope)   (far, away, gone)

37 (save, money, box)   (shop, keeper, spend)

38 (paint, brush, ugly)   (colour, pretty, box)

39 (pat, like, friend)   (unkind, sad, enemy)

40 (sound, quiet, song)   (noisy, voice, sang)   ⑤

Find and underline the two words which need to change places for each sentence to make sense.

Example   She went to <u>letter</u> the <u>write</u>.

41 We went to the year for our holiday this sea.

42 Mike likes to go to his grandmother's school after house.

43 I forgot that had I checked a book out of the library.

44 It is important to look ways both when crossing the street.

45 I planted some seeds in the garden that I'd grown from flowers.   ⑤

Complete the following sentences by selecting the most sensible word from each group of words given in the brackets. Underline the words selected.

Example The (<u>children</u>, books, foxes) carried the (houses, <u>books</u>, steps) home from the (greengrocer, <u>library</u>, factory).

1 She was very (cross, tired, glad) and said (she, he, it) would like to (stand, sit, run) down.

2 My older (mother, aunt, sister) went to a (school, dance, bag) with her (suitcase, dog, boyfriend).

3 She (left, gave, ate) her (car, pancake, purse) in the (pond, sea, shop).

4 Can you (speak, tell, ring) for the (ambulance, trolley, driving) from your (free, mobile, call) phone?

5 After (breakfast, lunch, supper) the (keys, bikes, moon) came up in the (day, afternoon, sky).

5

Choose the word or phrase that makes each sentence true.

Example A LIBRARY always has (posters, a carpet, books, DVDs, stairs).

6 A FOREST always has (benches, a lake, paths, flowers, trees).

7 A PIG always has (a name, a tag, a sty, a tail, spots).

8 A HUSBAND is always a (father, man, worker, driver, golfer).

9 A NURSE always works (alone, in a hospital, with patients, at night, in a city).

10 A FLOWER always has (a smell, thorns, roots, two leaves, yellow petals).

5

Underline any word which has the same letter three times.

11	December	Saturday	appears	potato
12	sparrow	trick	eleven	herring
13	individual	indeed	lesson	ironing
14	shines	eatable	release	gossip
15	necessary	alabaster	awkward	series

5

If the code for PLEASED is $+ - \times \div = \times /$, what are the codes for the following words?

16 PLEAD _____ **17** APPLE _____ **18** PALE _____

What do these codes stand for?

19 $/ \div - \times$ _____ **20** $/ \times \times /$ _____

5

Remove one letter from the word in capital letters to leave a new word. The meaning of the new word is given in the clue.

Example   AUNT   an insect   *ant*

21 CREATE   a box   _____

22 SOLID   bought by someone   _____

23 WHOLE   an opening   _____

24 HEARD   not soft   _____

25 SUPPER   great   _____

5

Underline the word in the brackets closest in meaning to the word in capitals.

Example   UNHAPPY   (unkind   death   laughter   sad   friendly)

26 PUPILS   (teacher   parents   friends   children   neighbours)

27 FELT TIPS   (rulers   writing   books   paper   pens)

28 SOUNDS   (whispers   shouts   silence   noises   cries)

29 HOUSE   (office   shed   bungalow   castle   airport)

30 CHEST   (arm   leg   box   suitcase   crate)

5

Underline the pair of words most opposite in meaning.

Example   cup, mug   coffee, milk   hot, cold

31 beginning, end   unkind, stern   safe, alive

32 smooth, soft   open, closed   first, fast

33 pick, pack   high, low   short, call

34 strong, weak   up, above   eat, food

35 sleep, tired   noise, shout   quiet, loud

5

Find the three-letter word which can be added to the letters in capitals to make a new word. The new word will complete the sentence sensibly.

Example   The cat sprang onto the MO.   U̲S̲E̲

36 My FRIS are all coming to my party.   _____

37 Sixty MIES make an hour.   _____

38 The building is very new and MRN.   _____

39 We moved here three YS ago.   _____

40 The police are offering a RED of £1000.   _____   **5**

In each line, underline the word that uses only the first six letters of the alphabet.

41 bake   bread   feed   abbot

42 black   face   dear   bale

43 band   aces   bead   abbey

44 fade   dream   dare   bake

45 deep   beak   bill   add   **5**

Now go to the Progress Chart to record your score!   Total   **45**

Paper 17

Here is a weather chart showing hours of sunshine.

Average hours of sunshine per day

	Apr	May	Jun	July	Aug	Sept	Oct
Costa del Sol	8	10	11	11	11	9	7
Costa Brava	8	8	9	10	9	7	5
London	6	7	7	7	6	5	3

1 How many hours of sunshine should the Costa Brava have each day in July? ____

2 The Costa del Sol should get ____ hours of sunshine each day in August.

3 In July the Costa del Sol should have ____ hours of sunshine each day.

4 The Costa Brava should get ____ hours of sunshine each day in April.

5 London should get ____ hours of sunshine each day in October.   **5**

48

Underline the pair of words most opposite in meaning.

Example   cup, mug   coffee, milk   <u>hot, cold</u>

6	sand, beach	heavy, light	tired, sleepy
7	run, around	write, ink	here, there
8	better, best	whisper, shout	read, write
9	late, early	fish, meat	cat, dog
10	talk, speak	date, year	glad, sad

○ 5

Find the three-letter word which can be added to the letters in capitals to make a new word. The new word will complete the sentence sensibly.

Example   The cat sprang onto the MO.   <u>USE</u>

11   The runners RD each other to win.   _____

12   The PAR is a bird usually kept in a cage.   _____

13   'Do up the BUTS on your shirt!'   _____

14   Tim liked BN sugar on his cereal.   _____

15   Nishpa ENS the festival of Diwali.   _____

○ 5

Find the letter which will end the first word and start the second word.

Example   peac (<u>h</u>) ome

16 han (__) eal   17 mat (__) nds   18 sal (__) wo

19 duc (__) now   20 mas (__) rack

○ 5

Look at the first group of three words. The word in the middle has been made from the other two words. Complete the second group of three words in the same way, making a new word in the middle.

Example   PAIN   IN<u>TO</u>   <u>TO</u>OK   ALSO   <u>SOON</u>   ONLY

21	HOME	MEAN	ANTS	SANE	_____	STAY
22	GREY	EYES	ESPY	EACH	_____	INCH
23	WEST	WEAR	ARTS	BATH	_____	SHED
24	LARK	LINK	SING	BEST	_____	NEAR
25	FIRE	FISH	SHOP	BEAR	_____	STEW

○ 5

(49)

Underline the two words, one from each group, which are closest in meaning.

Example (race, shop, <u>start</u>) (finish, <u>begin</u>, end)

26 (fire, help, hinder) (call, after, aid)

27 (ruin, match, result) (mend, spoil, again)

28 (hate, angry, soft) (cross, hard, fallen)

29 (talk, chat, hear) (see, listen, cost)

30 (price, garment, till) (shop, label, cost)

5

Find the missing number by using the two numbers outside the brackets in the same way as the others sets of numbers.

Example 2 [8] 4 3 [18] 6 5 [25] 5

31 3 [9] 3 4 [8] 2 5 [__] 1 32 4 [5] 1 2 [7] 5 6 [__] 3

33 17 [3] 14 8 [3] 5 11 [__] 7 34 9 [12] 3 5 [12] 7 6 [__] 2

35 30 [6] 5 18 [6] 3 24 [__] 8

5

Underline the number that completes the sentence.

36 6 is to 36 as 7 is to (49, 28, 56)

37 12 is to 9 as 40 is to (12, 20, 30)

38 14 is to 21 as 21 is to (24, 28, 32)

39 4 is to 20 as 50 is to (80, 250, 100)

40 19 is to 38 as 38 is to (19, 76, 50)

5

Underline the word in brackets closest in meaning to the word in capitals.

Example UNHAPPY (unkind death laughter <u>sad</u> friendly)

41 PIP (fruit flower seed skin flesh)

42 FROSTY (cold snowy icy bright bitter)

43 SKID (roll trip slide tumble brake)

44 RAISE (upright tall lift drop collect)

45 LEAN (tilt bend fat hungry curve)

5

Now go to the Progress Chart to record your score! Total 45

50

1–5 Look at these groups of words.

Group A Kitchen things   Group B Languages

Group C Birds   Group D Animals

Choose the correct group for each of the words below. Write in the letter.

whisk __   camel __   Dutch __   scales __   gull __

German __   lamb __   recipe __   goose __   French __

(5)

Find the three-letter word which can be added to the letters in capitals to make a new word. The new word will complete the sentence sensibly.

Example   The cat sprang onto the MO.   <u>USE</u>

6 Have you seen the fish in the WR?   _____

7 He was wearing a stripy SF.   _____

8 You must SH the money with Nina.   _____

9 Put the HING out to dry on the line.   _____

10 No one saw him SL the money.   _____

(5)

Find the letter which will end the first word and start the second word.

Example   peac (<u>h</u>) ome

11 lan (__) own   12 fea (__) urn   13 gon (__) lass

14 sto (__) lace   15 rop (__) ar

(5)

Fill in the crosswords so that all the given words are included. You have been given one letter as a clue in each crossword.

16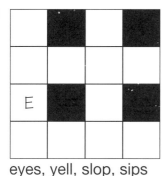

eyes, yell, slop, sips

17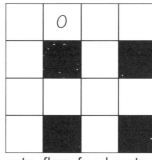

acts, flag, food, oats

(2)

Change the first word of the third pair in the same way as the other pairs to give a new word.

Example bind, hind   bare, hare   but, <u>hut</u>

18 and, sand   ill, sill   eat, _____

19 bet, best   cot, cost   lit, _____

20 cat, coat   bat, boat   mat, _____

21 fat, feat   mat, meat   hat, _____

22 is, this   at, that   an, _____   5

If the code for VEGETABLE is $+ / - / \times @ \$ = /$, what are the codes for the following words?

23 GET _____   24 BLEAT _____   25 LEAVE _____

What do these codes stand for?

26 $\times @ -$ _____   27 $- @ \times /$ _____   5

A and B wear blue jeans. C and B wear red shirts. D and A wear green shirts. C and D wear black jeans.

28 Who wore blue jeans and a red shirt?   —

29 Who wore black jeans and a green shirt?   —

30 Who wore blue jeans and a green shirt?   —

31 Who wore black jeans and a red shirt?   —   4

32 In each line, underline the word that uses only the first six letters of the alphabet.

dear   cedar   bead   feast   aside   1

If the following letters were arranged in alphabetical order, which letter comes in the middle?

33 CRIED   _____

34 BROKE   _____

35 SWEPT   _____   3

52

Complete the following sentences by selecting the most sensible word from each group of words given in the brackets. Underline the words selected.

Example The (<u>children</u>, books, foxes) carried the (houses, <u>books</u>, steps) home from the (greengrocer, <u>library</u>, factory).

36 I studied my (words, letters, numbers) because we had a (running, art, spelling) test at (home, school, camp).

37 The (painter, butcher, writer) worked alone in her (car, study, desk) trying to finish her (poet, works, book).

38 When the plane (landed, swam, ran) we (waved, broke, dropped) into (silence, applause, cheers).

39 My (sister, brother, father) got a ring from her (cat, boyfriend, baby) for her (lunch, job, birthday).

40 The actress (found, lost, spent) the (second, weekend, years) learning her (lines, characters, costume).

5

Underline the pair of words most similar in meaning.

Example come, go   <u>roam, wander</u>   fear, fare

41 leave, depart   run, sit   sleep, awake

42 rough, smooth   half, whole   bitter, sour

43 messy, neat   calm, peaceful   rude, polite

44 sweep, brush   loose, tight   hungry, full

45 straight, crooked   grateful, thankful   less, more

5

Now go to the Progress Chart to record your score!   Total   45

Paper 19

Underline the word in brackets closest in meaning to the word in capitals.

Example UNHAPPY   (unkind   death   laughter   <u>sad</u>   friendly)

1 SIMILAR   (different   wrong   same   familiar   smile)

2 TALK   (shout   say   whisper   argue   cry)

3 ALLOW   (stop   low   ask   let   all)

4 DEAR   (sweet   light   honest   dare   beloved)

5 BEECH   (sand   sea   tree   plant   branch)   5

Find the three-letter word which can be added to the letters in capitals to make a new word. The new word will complete the sentence sensibly.

Example   The cat sprang onto the MO.   U<u>SE</u>

6 The tennis CTS were fully booked.   _____

7 The police issued a WART for his arrest.   _____

8 My sister wears ARMDS for swimming.   _____

9 When the sun shines I can see my SOW.   _____

10 I need to SHAR my pencil.   _____   5

Find the letter which will end the first word and start the second word.

Example   peac (<u>h</u>) ome

11 gat (__) ase

12 min (__) act

13 zon (__) tch

14 ben (__) rim

15 als (__) dds   5

Give the missing groups of letters and numbers in the following sequences. The alphabet has been written out to help you.

A B C D E F G H I J K L M N O P Q R S T U V W X Y Z

Example   CQ   DP   EQ   FP   <u>GQ</u>

16 AZ   DY   GX   JW   ____

17 2B   4D   6F   ____   10J

18 ____   CDF   EFH   GHJ   IJL

19 Ma   ____   Oc   Pd   Qe

20 9ZY   8XW   ____   6TS   5RQ   5

Fill in the crosswords so that all the given words are included. You have been given one letter as a clue in each crossword.

21

22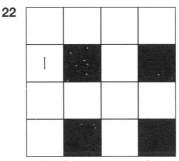

dale, leap, alas, deal

pain, into, note, pint

23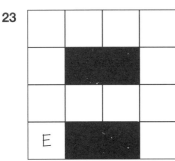

slow, site, week, type

3

Rearrange the muddled letters in capitals to make a proper word. The answer will complete the sentence sensibly.

Example A BEZAR is an animal with stripes. _ZEBRA_

24 We came at last to the ALECST gate. _____

25 Has AOEYNN seen my pen? _____

26 The IPREAT had a bag of money and a parrot. _____

27 We're going to the NICEAM tomorrow evening. _____

28 Please can you do the GNIPOPSH today? _____

5

These words have been written in code, but the codes are not under the right words.

TOP	POT	TOO	TON	NOTE
6417	144	146	541	145

Write the correct code for each word.

29 TOP   **30** POT   **31** TOO   **32** TON   **33** NOTE

_____   _____   _____   _____   _____

5

Complete the following sentences by selecting the most sensible word from each group of words given in the brackets. Underline the words selected.

> **Example** The (children, books, foxes) carried the (houses, books, steps) home from the (greengrocer, library, factory).

34 The (queen, king, prince) who lived in a (shed, train, castle) only wore her (hair, shoes, crown) for special occasions.

35 I set my alarm (pen, torch, clock) for seven o'clock because I wanted to be (on time, late, known) for my first day at (school, moon, tea).

36 During the (summer, winter, autumn) we sometimes get (snow, rain, clouds) which means we get to go (sledging, eating, sun bathing).

37 When I feel (well, ill, happy) my grandmother gives me some (medicine, trousers, glasses) to help me feel (sad, worse, better).

4

Remove one letter from the word in capital letters to leave a new word. The meaning of the new word is given in the clue.

> **Example** AUNT an insect _ant_

38 SNAP   a rest   _____

39 SPEND   to tell to go   _____

40 SPOKE   to push or jab   _____

41 SPOIL   dirt or earth   _____

42 HAUNT   a relative   _____

5

If the word DAUGHTERS is written in code as 123456789, what is the sum of these words?

43 D + A + T + E = _____

44 R + E + A + D = _____

45 T + R + E + E = _____

3

Paper 20

Complete these questions. The alphabet has been given to help you.

A B C D E F G H I J K L M N O P Q R S T U V W X Y Z

Example AB is to CD as PQ is to RS.

1 A35 is to B40 as C45 is to ____.

2 29A is to 31B as 33C is to ____.

3 AZ is to BY as CX is to ____.

4 AB is to CD as EF is to ____.

5 W is to V as U is to ____.

Fill in the missing number in each sequence.

Example 2 4 6 8 <u>10</u>

6 1 2 4 7 ___

7 40 36 ___ 28 24

8 5 10 15 ___ 25

9 24 21 ___ 15 12

10 7 14 21 28 ___

These words have been written in code, but the codes are not under the correct words. One code is missing.

RAN	ADD	RAIN	RING	AND
4751	4275	256	266	

Write the correct code for each word.

11 RAN   12 ADD   13 RAIN   14 RING   15 AND

____   ____   ____   ____   ____

If the word MARIGOLD is written in code as 12345678, what is the sum of these words?

16 G + O + L + D = ____   17 G + R + I + M = ____

18 L + A + I + R = ____

Underline the two words which are made from the same letters.

Example   TAP   PET   <u>TEA</u>   POT   <u>EAT</u>

19 INCH   CHAP   CHIN   NICE   PACK

20 CRUSH   SHUSH   BRUSH   SHRUB   BUNCH

21 RAIN   NEAT   NEAR   EARN   TENT

22 CLASP   CLASS   SCORE   PLACE   SCALP

4

Change one word so that the sentence makes sense. Underline the word you are taking out and write your new word on the line.

Example   I waited in line to buy a <u>book</u> to see the film.   *ticket*

23 I ran out of toothpaste so couldn't brush my feet.   _____

24 The pig barked to be let into the house.   _____

25 'It isn't my reason that the window is broken!'   _____

3

Underline the pair of words most similar in meaning.

Example   come, go   <u>roam, wander</u>   fear, fare

26 young, old   brief, short   good, bad

27 in, out   better, worse   glad, happy

28 dark, light   yell, scream   colour, plain

29 talk, speak   cold, hot   bed, time

30 read, story   see, look   eat, food

5

Find the three-letter word which can be added to the letters in capitals to make a new word. The new word will complete the sentence sensibly.

Example   The cat sprang onto the MO.   <u>USE</u>

31 We TLED through the crowds.   _____

32 The SPACES landed on the moon.   _____

33 The eagle SED effortlessly.   _____

34 We FOLED the path to the sea.   _____

35 The player SCO a goal.   _____

5

Find the letter which will end the first word and start the second word.

Example peac (h) ome

36 hai (—) ean 37 mos (—) ime

38 pai (—) rip 39 bel (—) hen

40 cak (—) ven

Underline two words, one from each group, that go together to form a new word. The word in the first group always comes first.

Example (hand, green, for) (light, house, sure)

41 (birth, help, cradle) (less, more, much)

42 (pick, slow, set) (end, back, forward)

43 (in, smoke, match) (fire, water, stick)

44 (dirty, mess, clean) (time, old, age)

45 (let, come, in) (room, doors, stairs)

Now go to the Progress Chart to record your score! Total 45

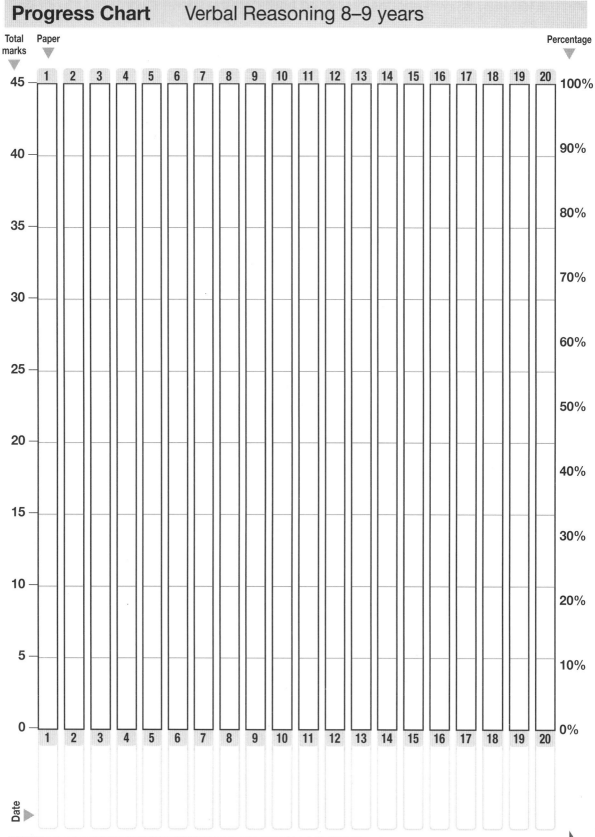

Progress Chart   Verbal Reasoning 8–9 years

When you've finished the book use the Next Steps Planner